We dedicate this book to Jack and Lucy,
their birth mothers and our mothers.

Cattleya trianae or Flor de Mayo

The national flower of Colombia

BunnyScooter

Bunny Scooter, LLC
bunnyscooter1@gmail.com

Born in Colombia

Book design by Monica Rickert-Bolter

ISBN 978-1-7369454-0-7
LCCNN: 2021911803

Publisher's Cataloging-In-Publication Data
(Prepared by The Donohue Group, Inc.)

Names: Creighton, Susan, 1958- author. | Mattimore, Colleen,
    author. | Hunt, Myles, illustrator.
Title: Born in Colombia / written by Susan Creighton and Colleen
    Mattimore ; illustrated by Myles Hunt.
Description: [East Aurora, New York] : Bunny Scooter, [2021] |
    Interest age level: 003-008. | Summary: Two children adopted
    from Colombia give an informative tour of their birth country.
    It highlights Colombia's geographic features, animals,
    industry and culture.
Identifiers: ISBN 9781736945407 | ISBN 9781736945414 (ebook)
Subjects: LCSH: Adopted children--Juvenile literature. | Colombia-
    -Description and travel--Juvenile literature. | Colombia--Social
    life and customs--Juvenile literature. | CYAC: Adopted children.
    | Colombia--Description and travel. | Colombia--Social life and
    customs.
Classification: LCC F2258.5 .C74 2021 (print) | LCC F2258.5 (ebook) |
    DDC 918.61 [E]--dc23

Born in Colombia

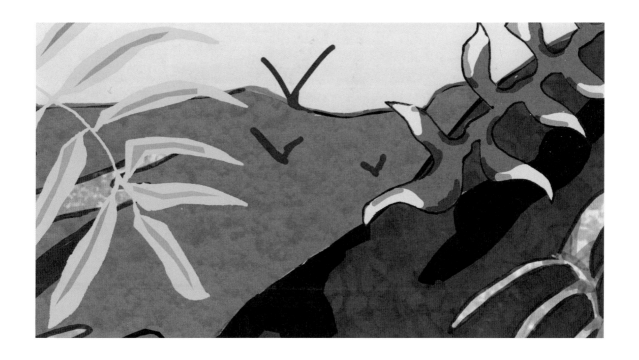

**Written by Susan Creighton
and Colleen Mattimore**

Illustrated by Myles Hunt

Our parents show us pictures and read us books about Colombia. We like hearing about it.

Because we were born there, we call it our birth county.

North

West — East

South

North
America

Europe

Asia

Africa

South
America

Australia

Colombia!

Antarctica

Did you know that Colombia is the fourth largest country on the continent of
South America?

amazing rainforests...

Because Colombia is so close to the Equator, the weather is warm all year long.

Sometimes it's sunny, sometimes it's cloudy and sometimes it rains a lot...

but it almost never snows.

Equator

The mountains and rainforests are home to many amazing animals like armadillos, spectacled bears and jaguars.

Spectacled bears are special and rare.

Did you know they are called spectacled bears because they look like they are wearing glasses?

Some say there are more kinds of plants in Colombia than anywhere else on earth.

Vegetables, fruits and flowers that grow there are sent all over the world.

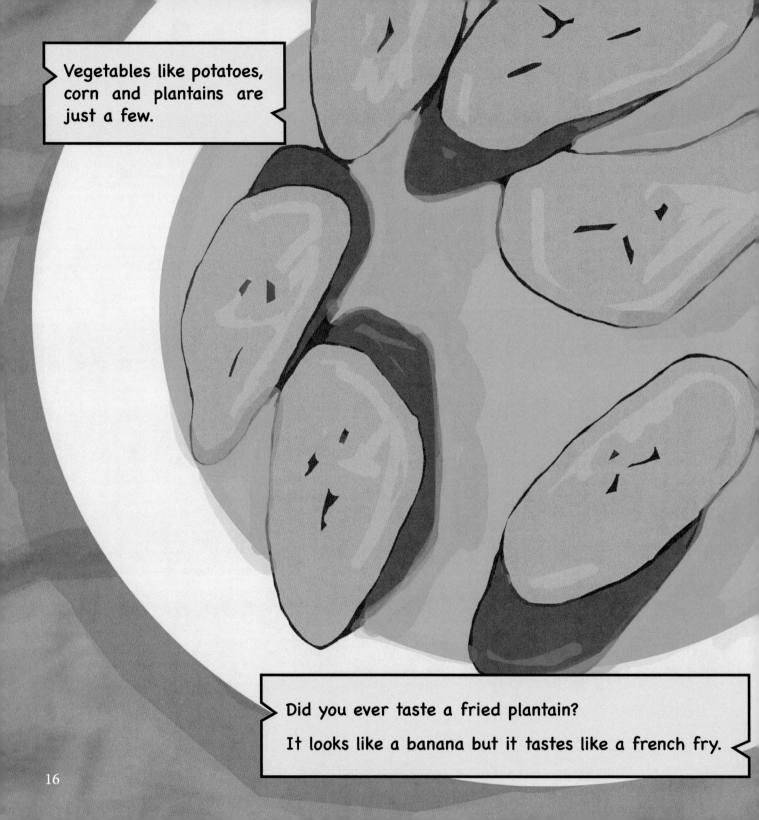

Vegetables like potatoes, corn and plantains are just a few.

Did you ever taste a fried plantain?

It looks like a banana but it tastes like a french fry.

Some fruits that grow in Colombia are... mango, guava and bananas.

17

And flowers, like roses, sunflowers and tulips come from Colombia too.

The next time you smell a rose stop and think... it might be from Colombia.

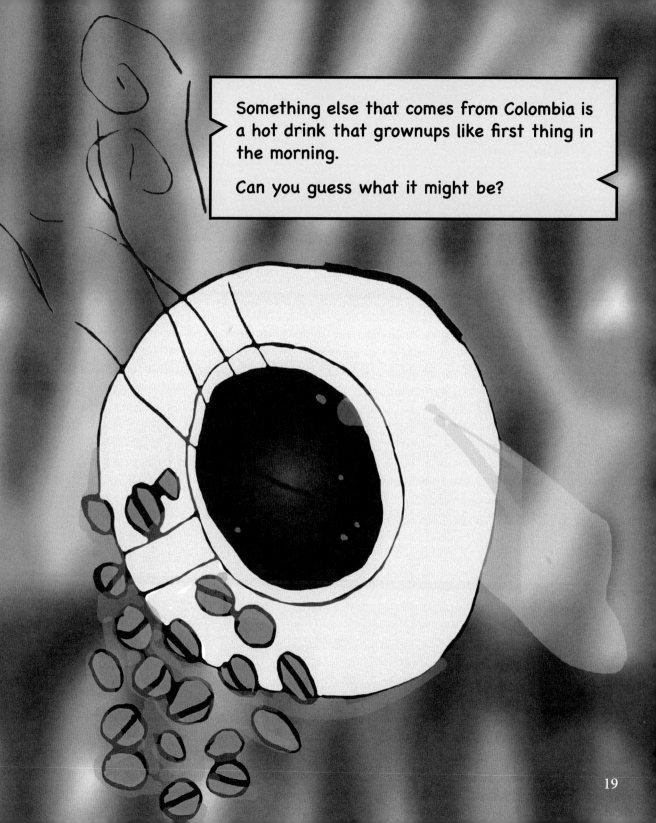

Something else that comes from Colombia is a hot drink that grownups like first thing in the morning.

Can you guess what it might be?

If you guessed COFFEE, you're right!

People who live in Colombia speak Spanish.

We like to say Spanish words and practice speaking Spanish with each other.

21

Colombian people come in all sizes, shapes and colors. Some are tall and some are short. Some have tan skin, black hair and brown eyes and some have light skin, blonde hair and green eyes. No matter what they look like, they are all Colombian.

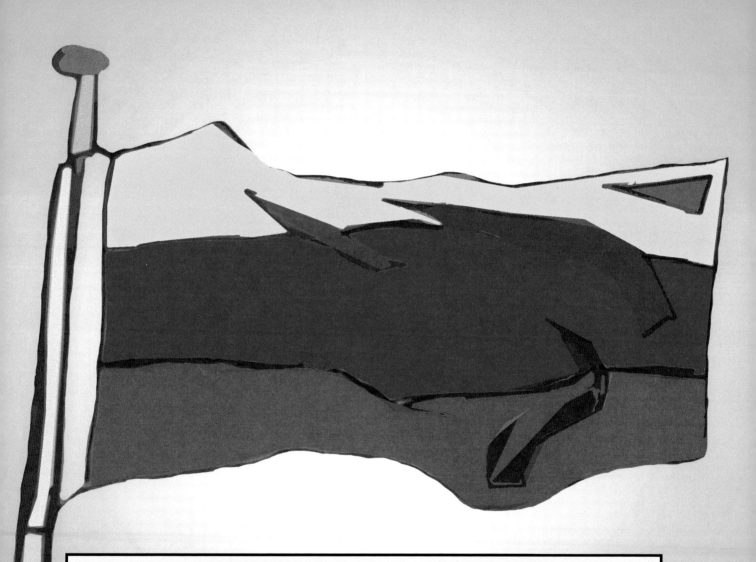

The people have festivals, carnivals and fairs throughout the year.

They celebrate their Independence Day on July 20th.

The flag of Colombia is yellow, blue and red.

Food & Drink

Colombians celebrate with festive music, dancing and delicious food.

They eat empanadas and drink juices made from fresh fruit.

24

25

There are many emerald mines in Colombia. Emeralds are shiny, green gem stones.

Soccer is a popular sport in Colombia.

Most kids learn how to play when they are very young.

We like to play soccer too.

We feel special being from Colombia and can't wait to go and visit someday.

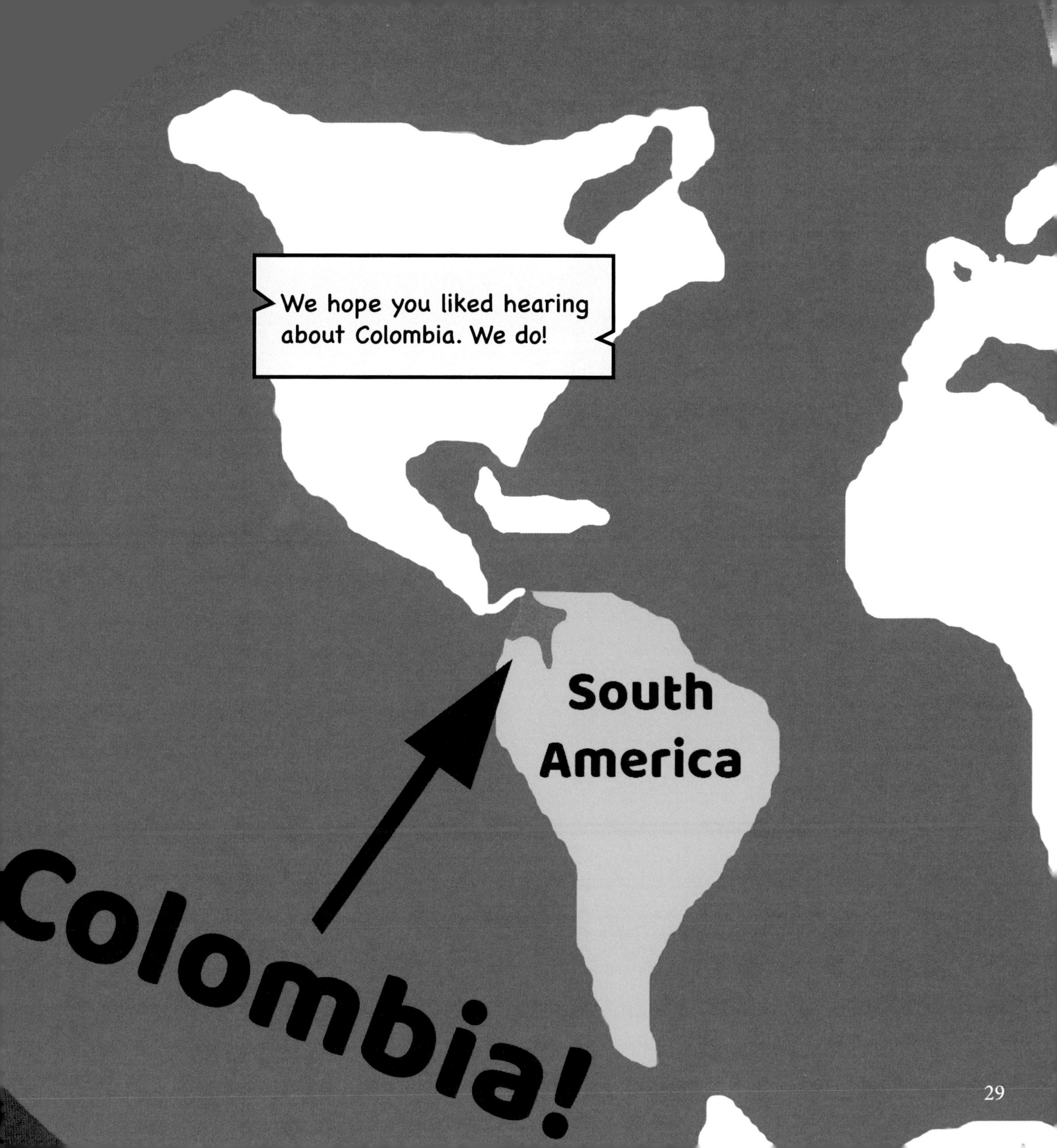
We hope you liked hearing about Colombia. We do!
South America
Colombia!

We like knowing about the rainforest and the animals.

And about the people and the flag.

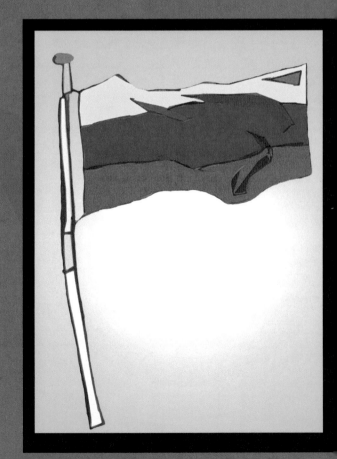

And about how a lot of wonderful things come from Colombia like delicious fruits,

beautiful flowers,

tasty coffee...

and us... Jack and Lucy! "ADIOS!"

Glossary

RAINFOREST
Woodland with very tall trees, found in tropical areas, where it rains often.

EQUATOR
An imaginary circle around the middle of the earth. It divides the earth in half; the northern hemisphere and the southern hemisphere.

TROPICAL
Land near the equator that has a warm climate.

BOGOTA
The capital city of Colombia. It is the biggest city in Colombia and over 8 million people live there. It has many universities, libraries and beautiful parks.

EMPANADAS
A pastry either baked or fried. It can be filled with either meat or potatoes or fruit.

PLANTAIN
A food like a banana, served at many meals. It is usually cooked before eating; they can also be deep fried and served like chips.

33

About the Authors

Susan Creighton, DTR, is a registered dance therapist and child mental health specialist. She has an MA in Creative Arts Therapies from NYU and spent her clinical career working with children and families. She has developed plans, programs and now a children's picture book series to provide tools and experiences for children to grow, explore and feel better. Sue is the proud mother of Lucy and Patrick; both were internationally adopted.

Colleen Mattimore, MD, FAAP, is a practicing pediatrician in Western New York. A recognized vaccine champion, she is an active member of the American Academy of Pediatrics and the Buffalo Pediatric Society. She promotes literacy and early reading through the Reach Out and Read Program. Colleen is the proud mother of three children, one born in Colombia.

About the Illustrator

Myles Hunt is a proud hearing aid wearer and visual artist residing in Brooklyn, NY. His work ranges from illustration, oil & acrylic painting, metalwork, puppetry, illustration and collage. The aesthetic he brings to his world matches his love for color and optimistic vibrancy.

Made in the USA
Monee, IL
23 April 2022

95234327R00024